Copyright © 2021
All rights reserved.

No part of this publication may be reproduced, distributed or transmitted in any form or by any means including photocopying, recording or other electronic or mechanical methods, without permission of the publisher, except in the case of brief quotations embodied in critical reviews and certain other non-commercial uses permitted by copyright law.

All rights reserved.

AFRICAN AMERICAN COLORING BOOKS FOR KIDS

A coloring book with positive affirmations of confidence, self-love and gratitude for black children

THIS BOOK BELONGS TO:

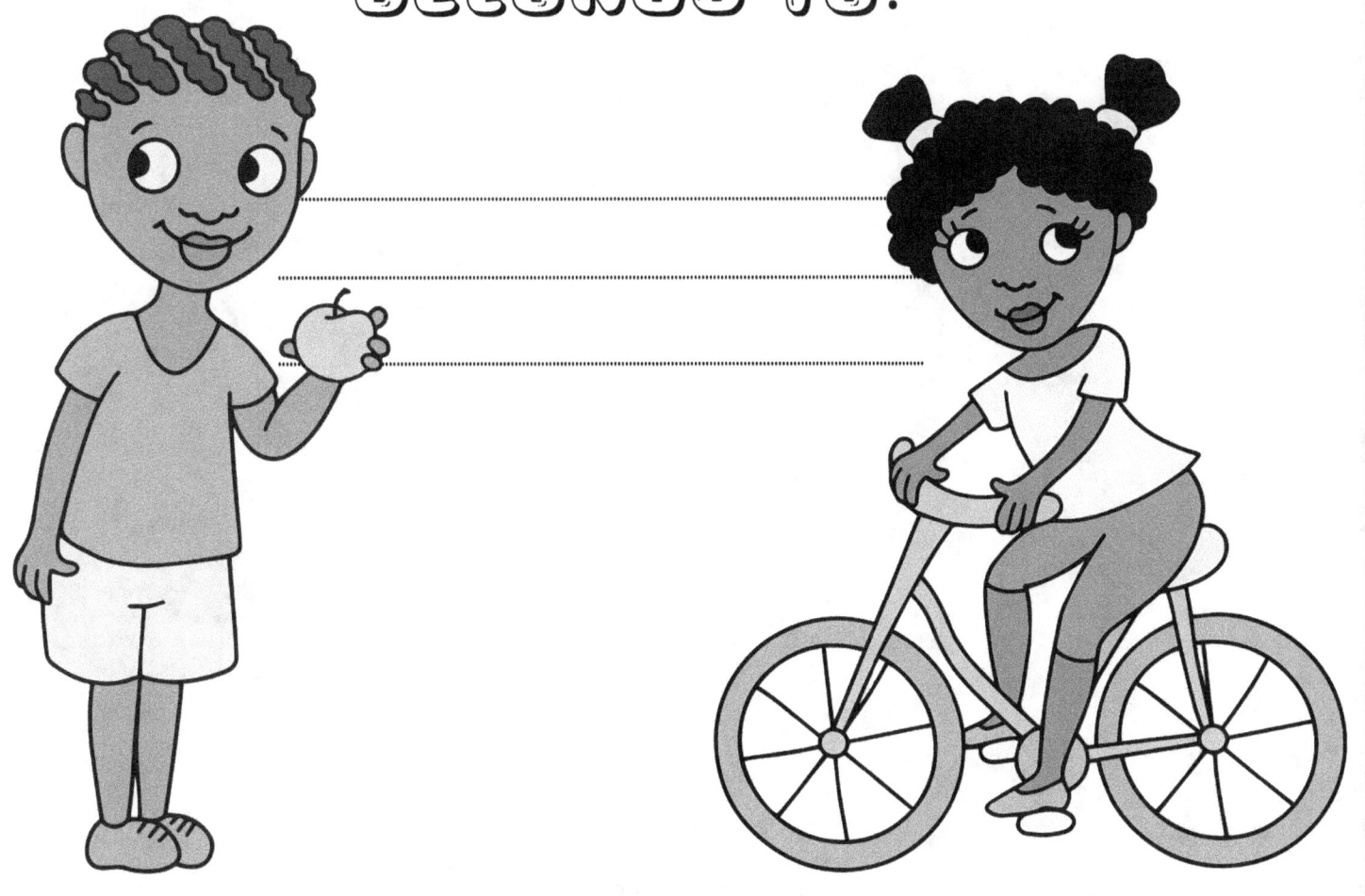

All rights reserved.

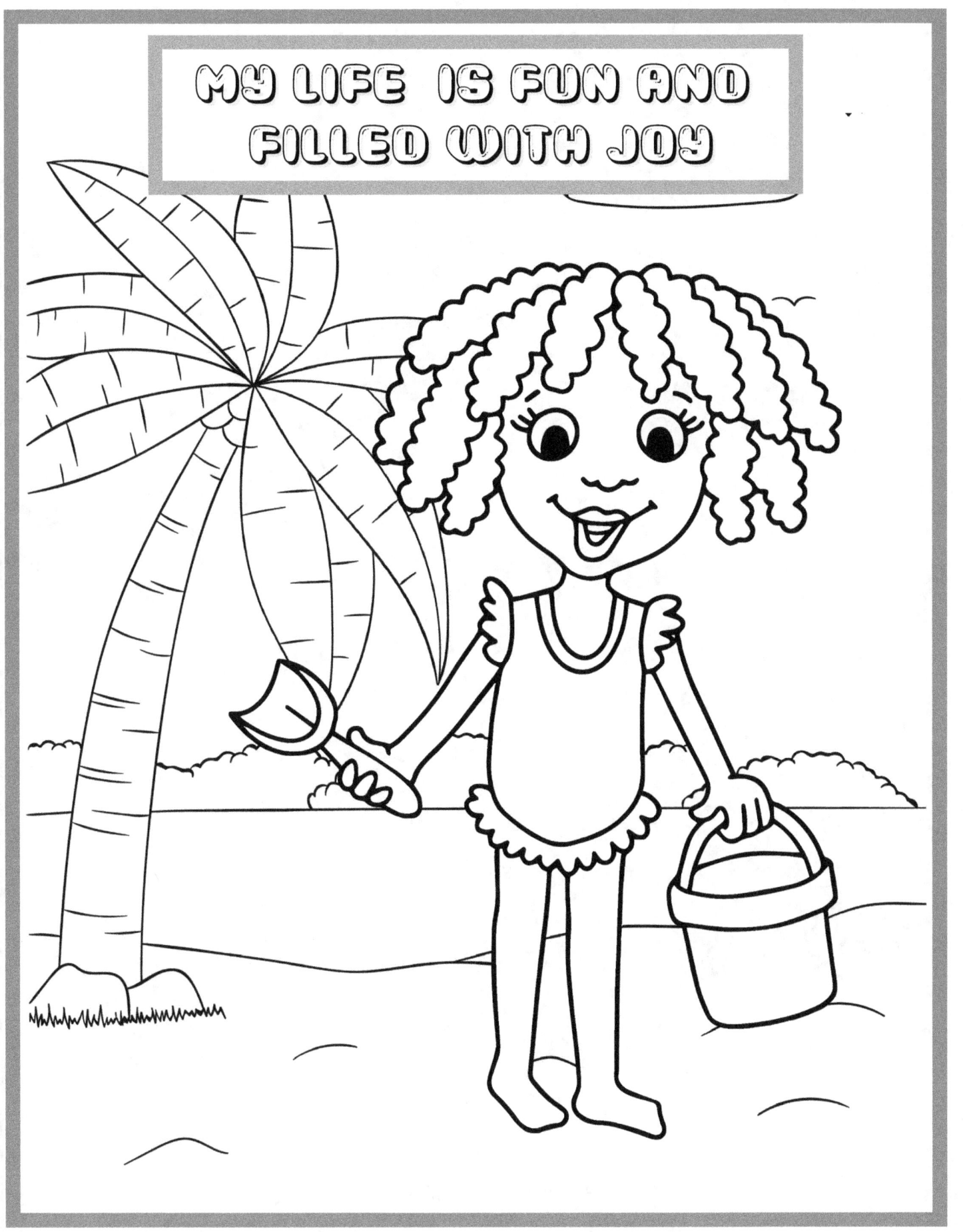

All rights reserved.

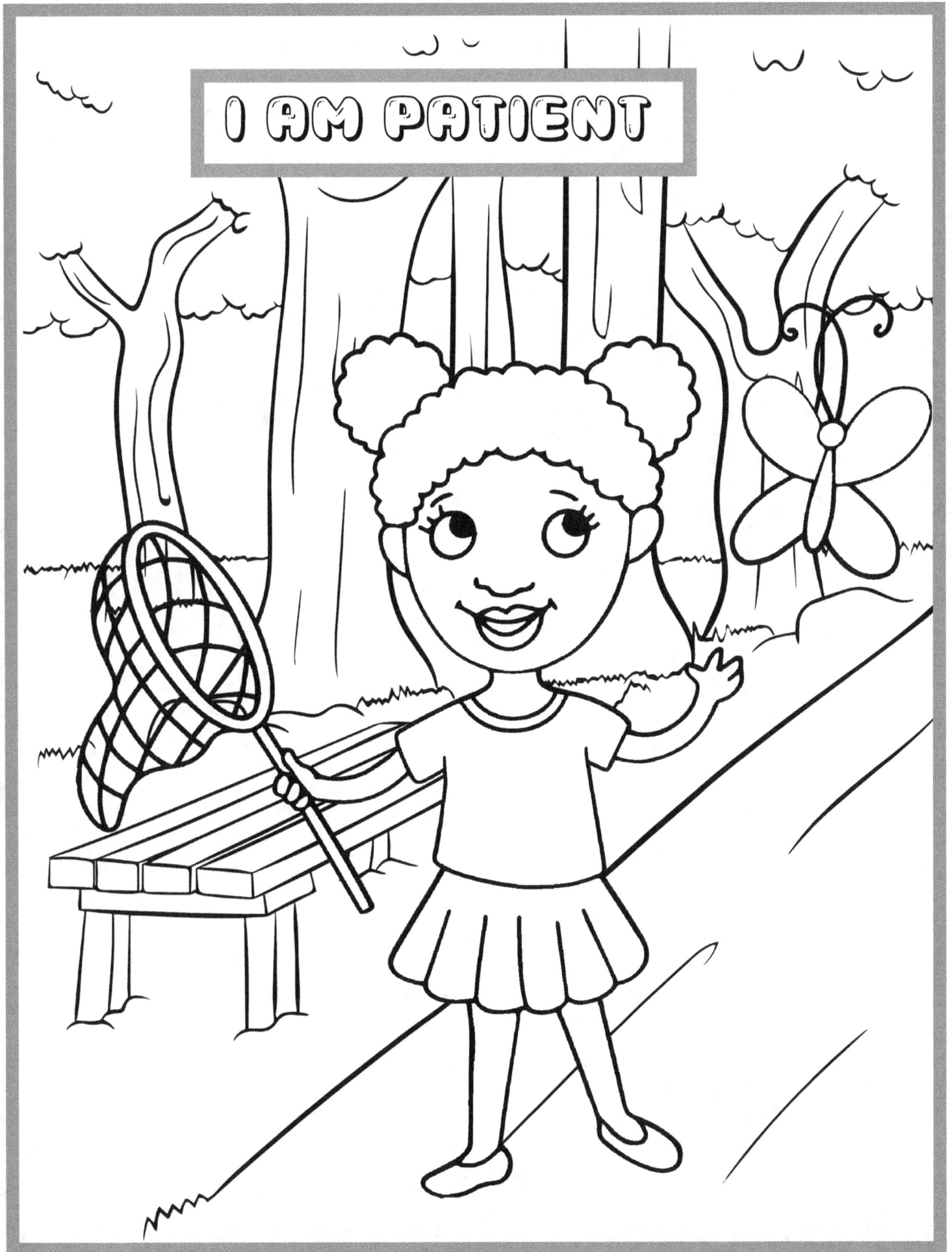

All rights reserved.

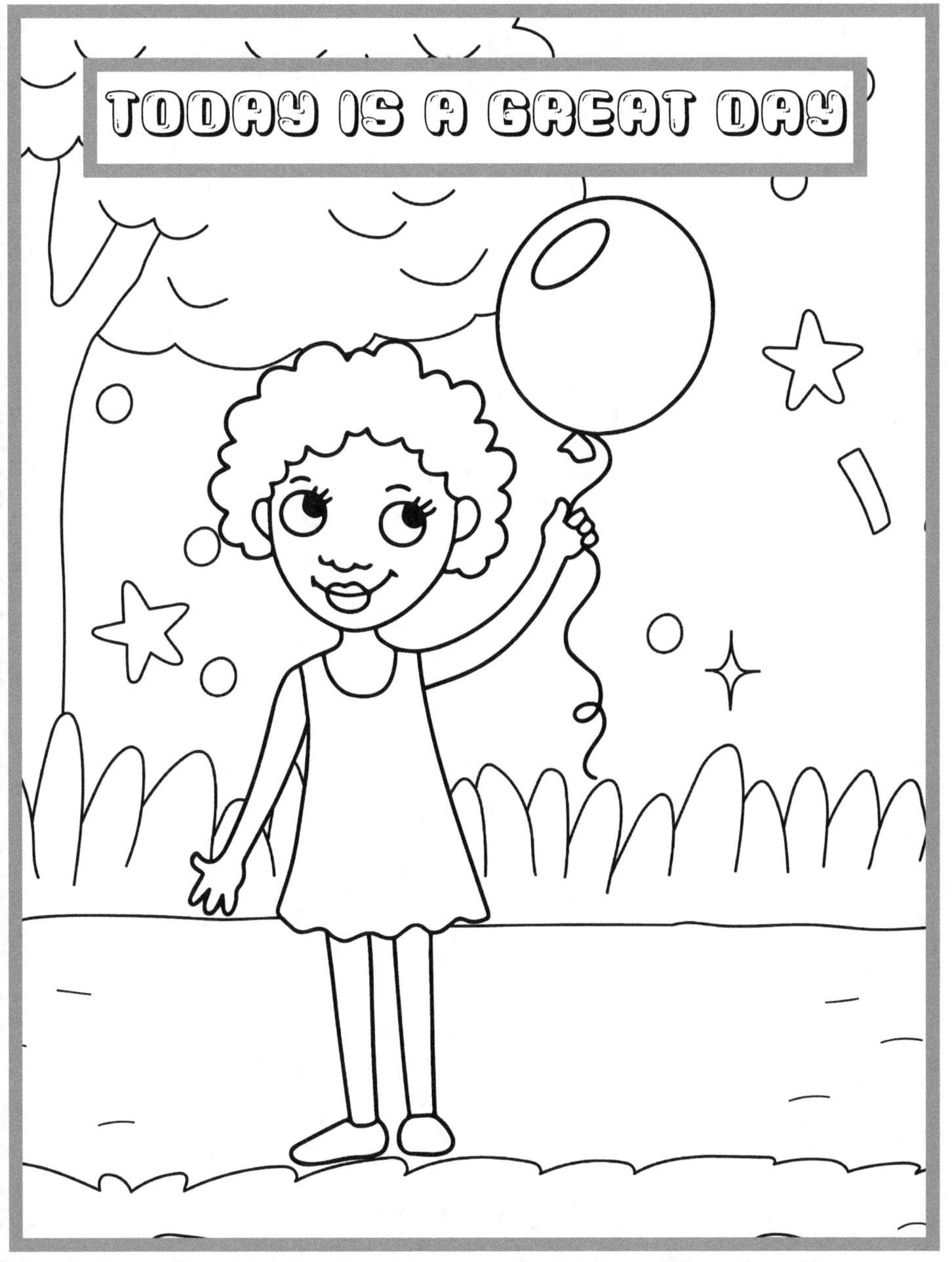

All rights reserved.

I LOVE TRYING NEW THINGS

All rights reserved.

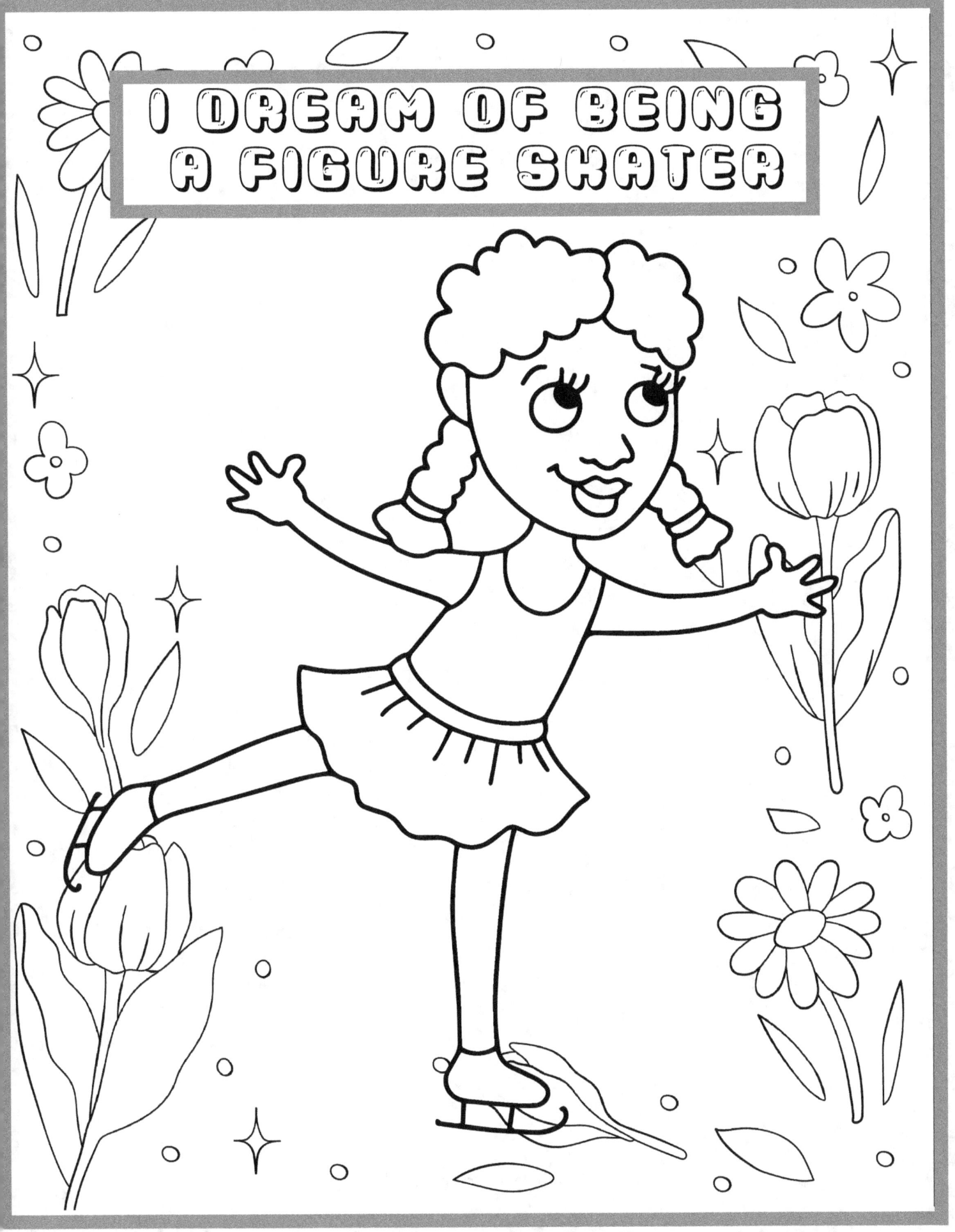

All rights reserved.

COACH ME AND I WILL LEARN

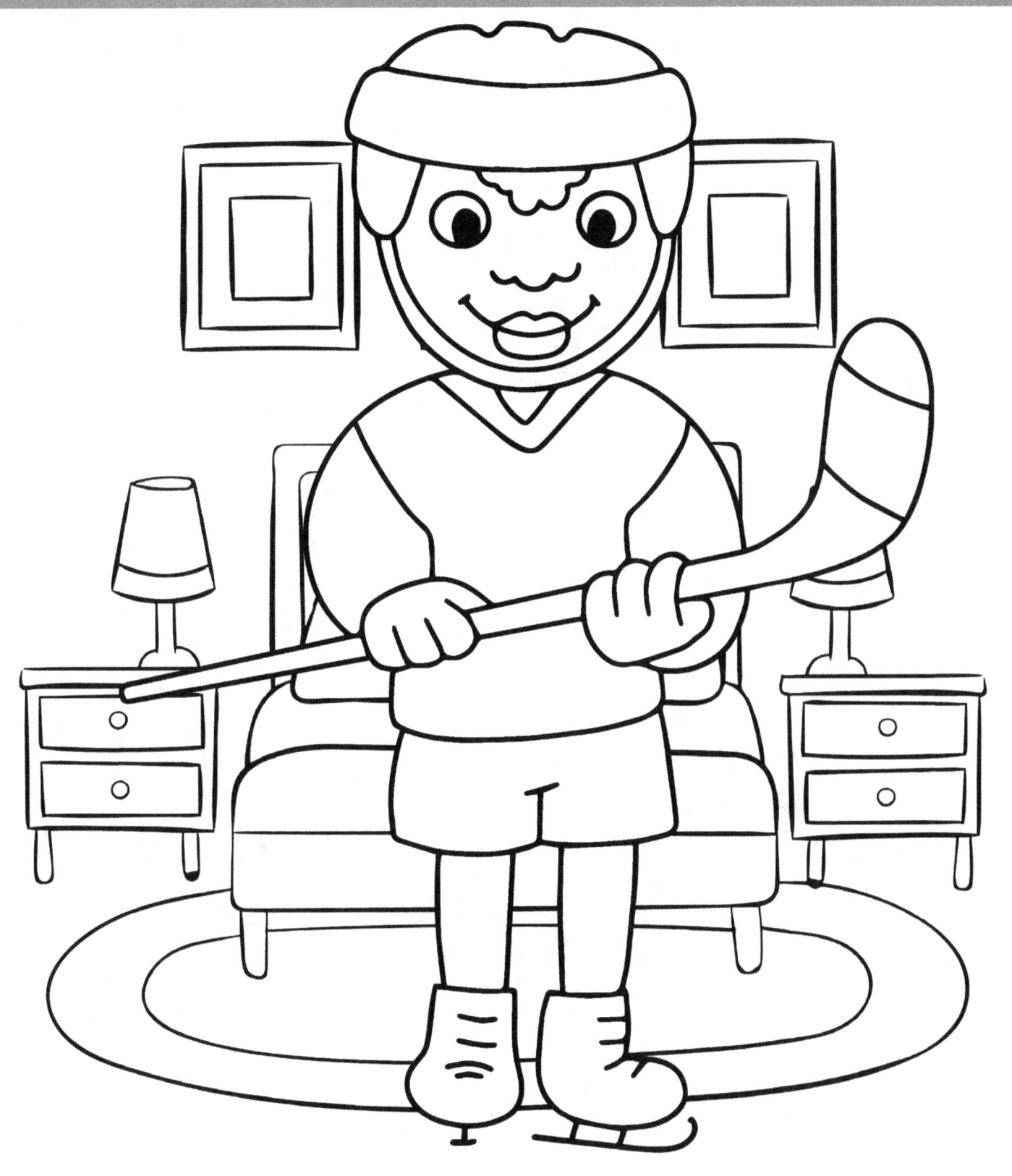

All rights reserved.

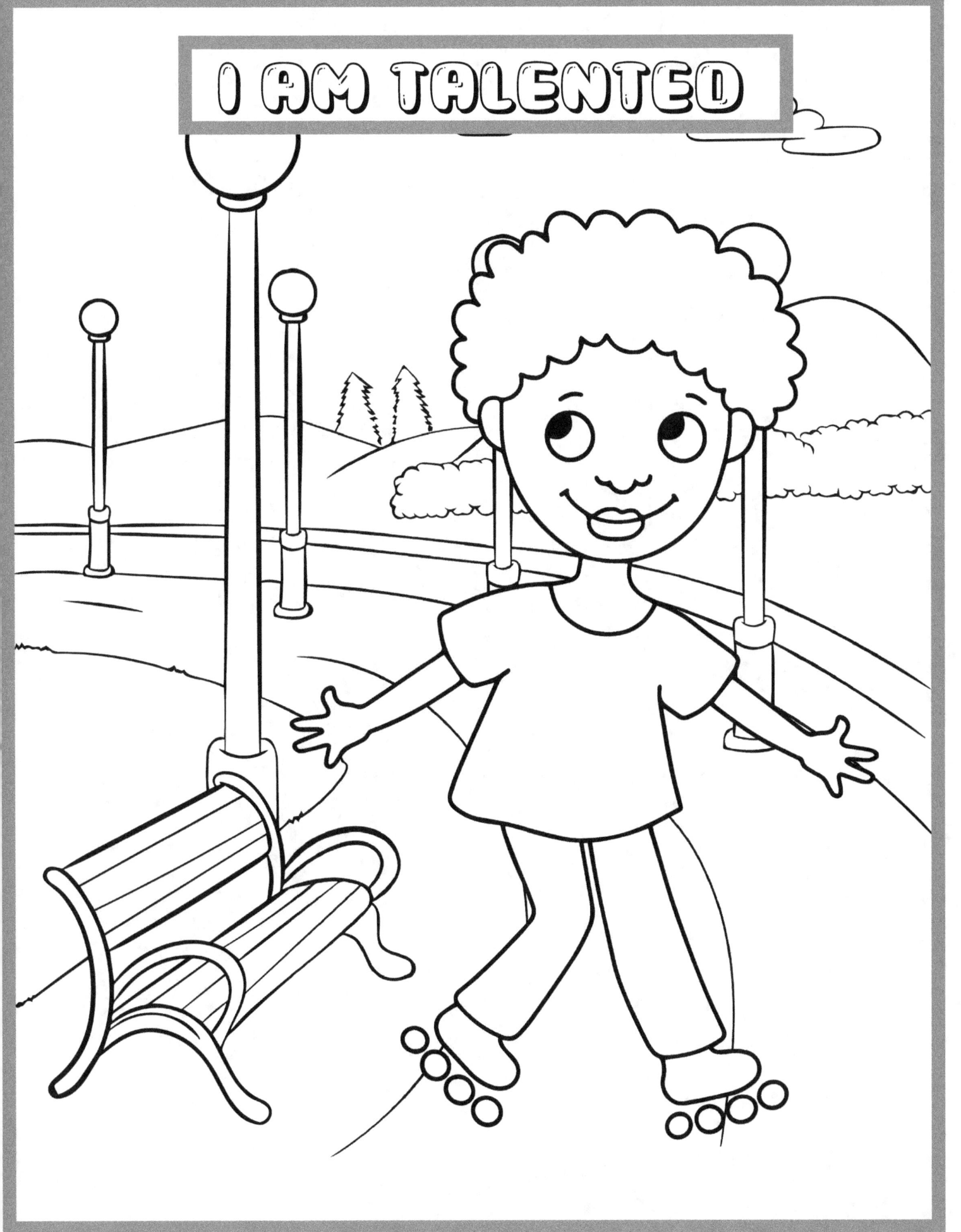

All rights reserved.

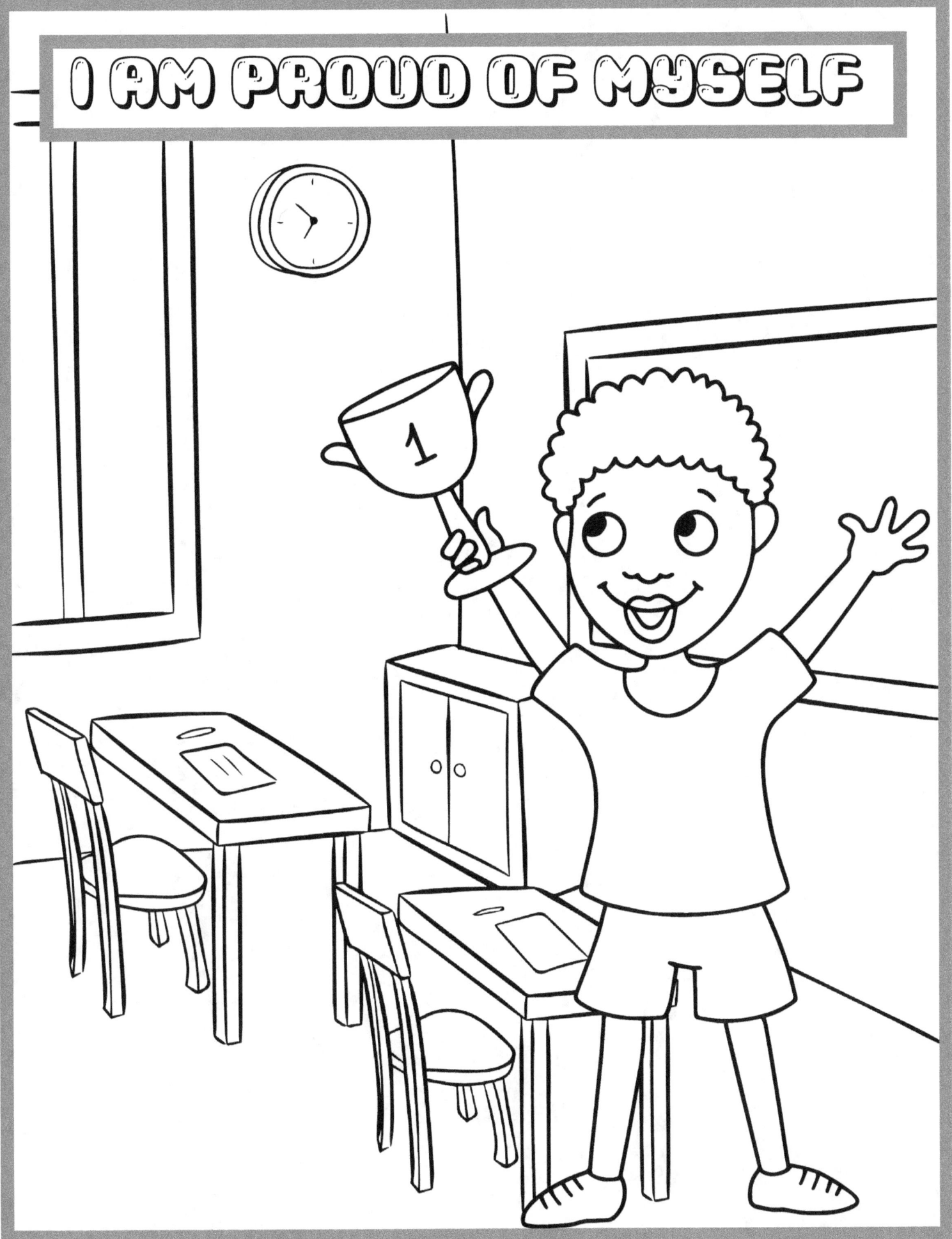

All rights reserved.

I CAN TAKE CARE OF MYSELF

All rights reserved.

I EAT HEALTHY SNACKS

All rights reserved.

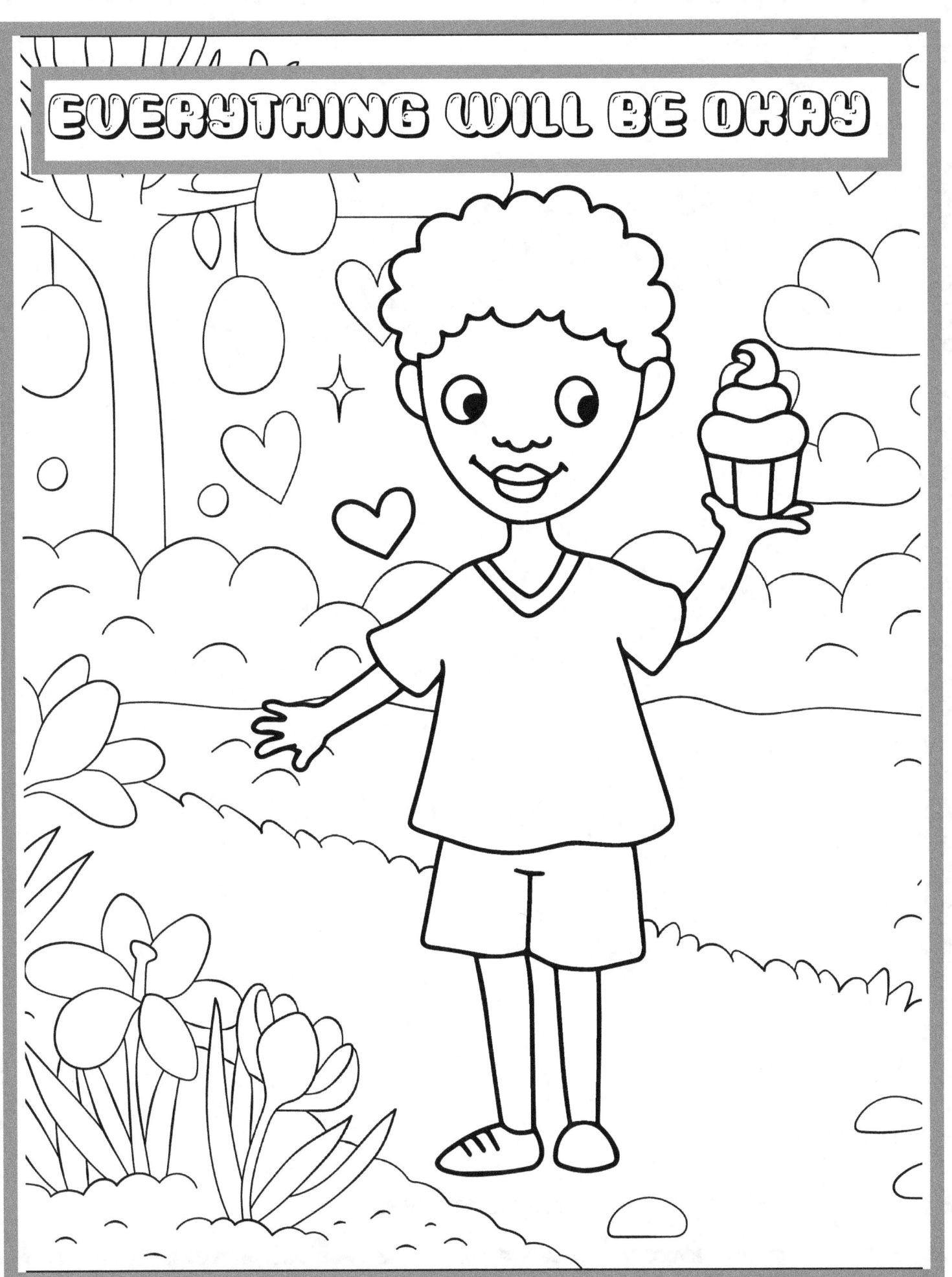

All rights reserved.

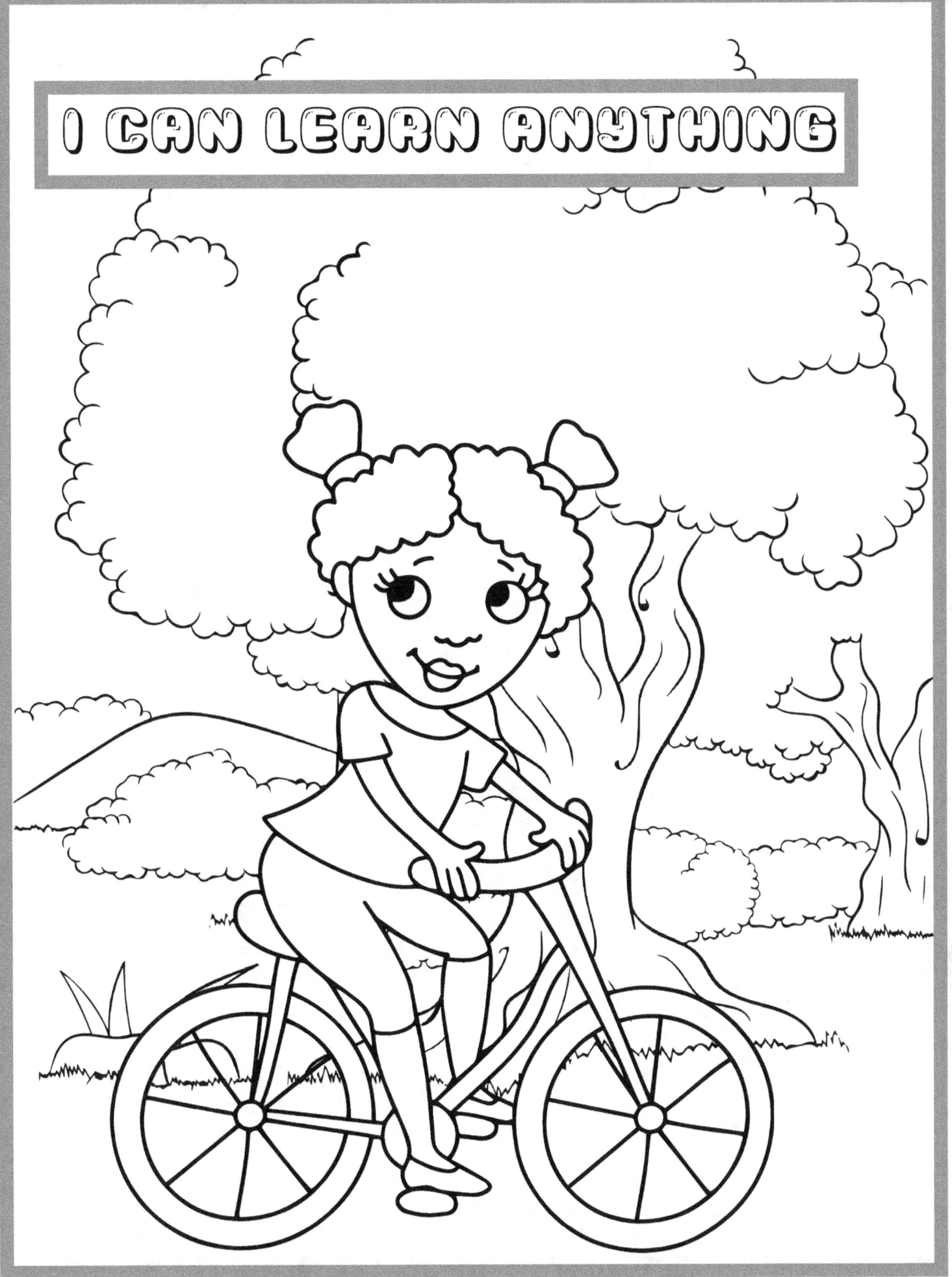

All rights reserved.

IT IS ENOUGH TO DO MY BEST

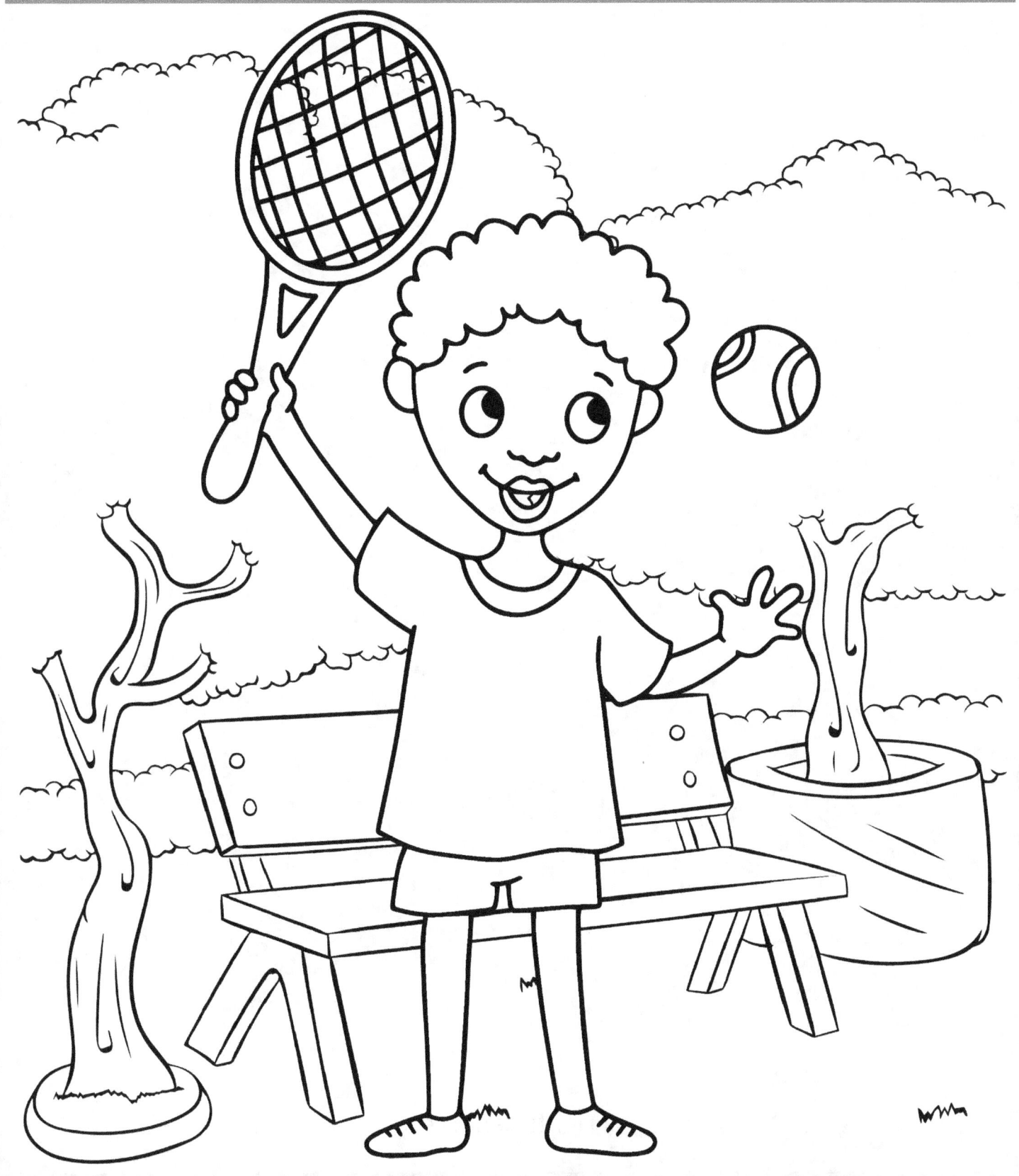

All rights reserved.

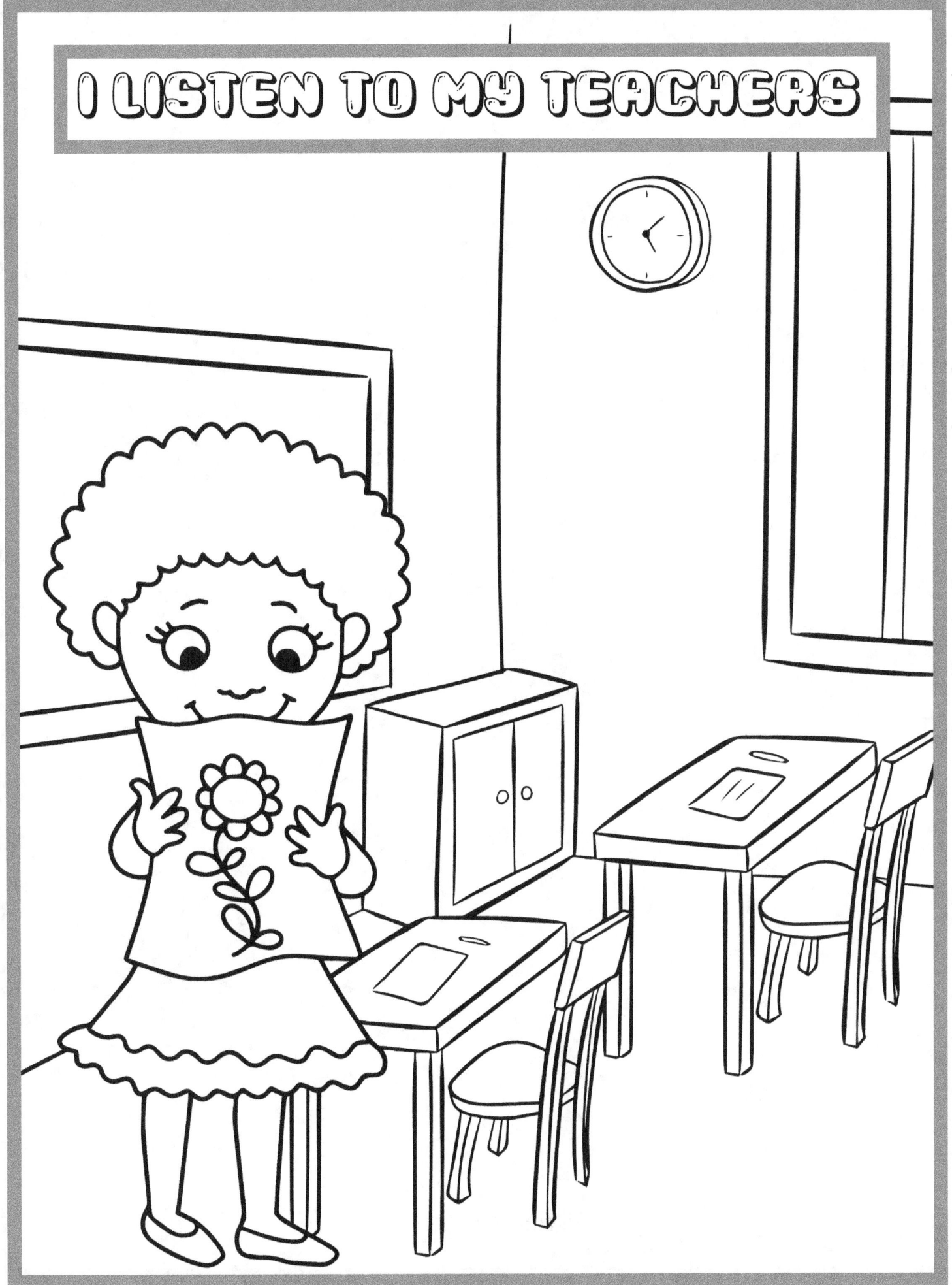

All rights reserved.

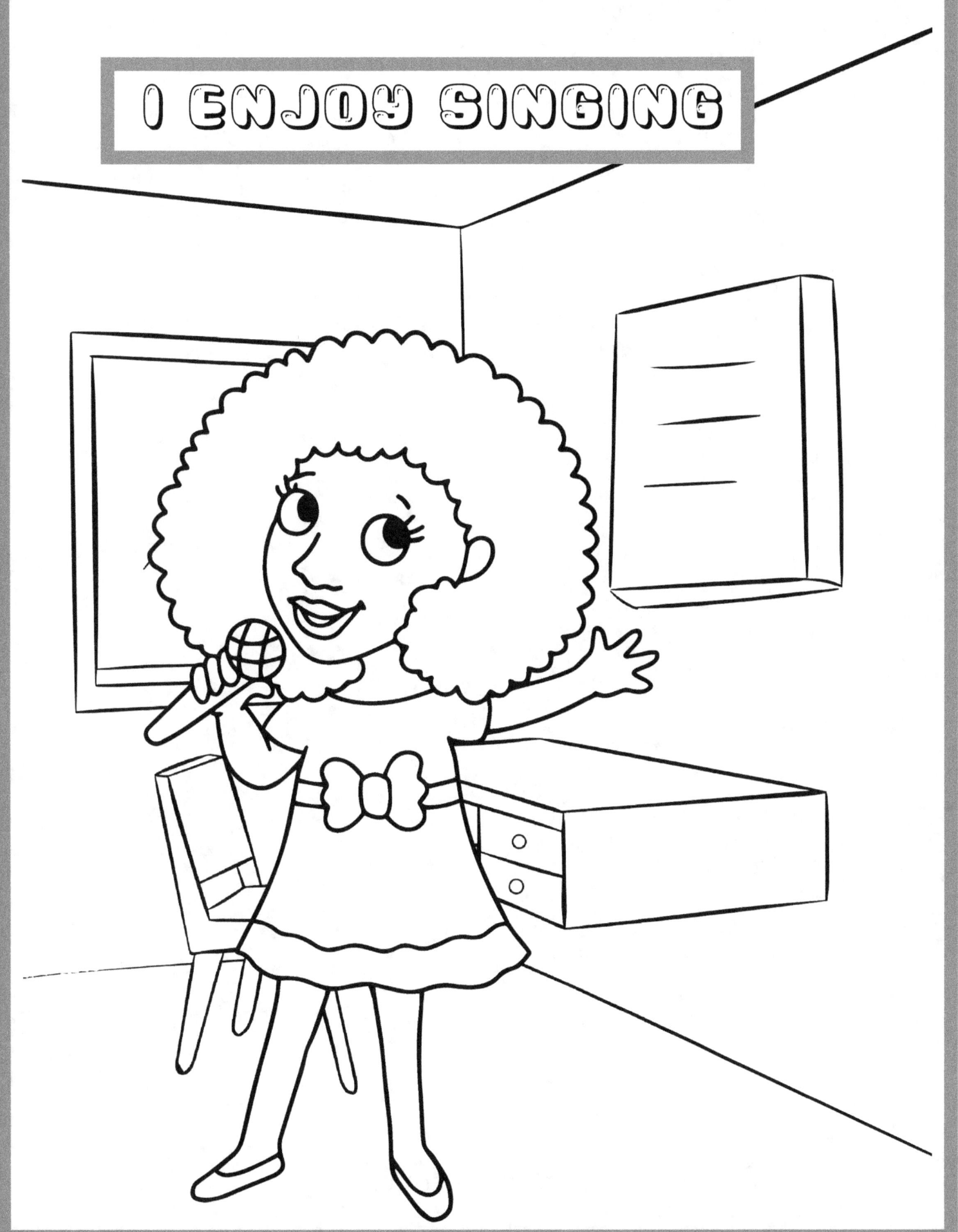

All rights reserved.

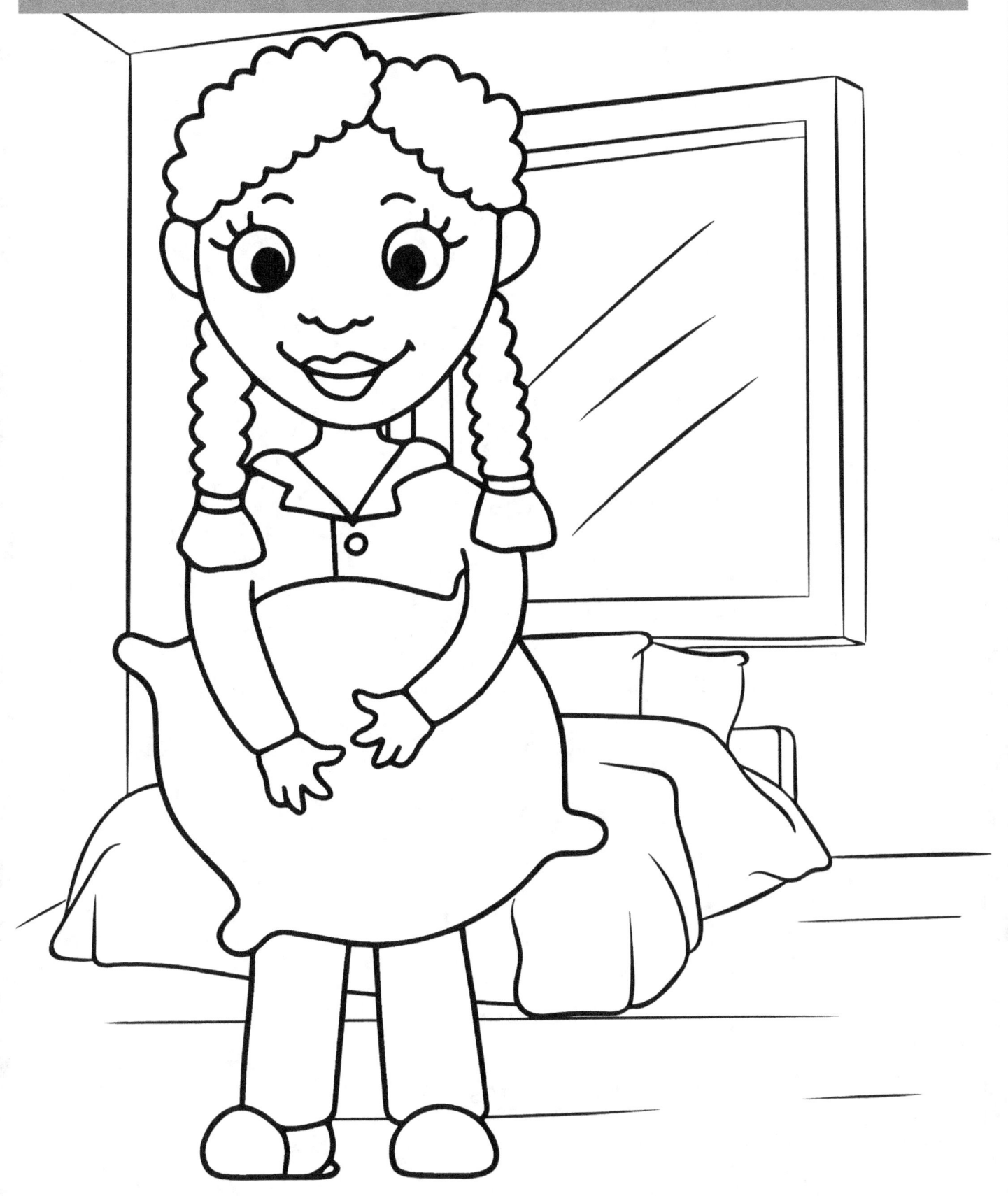
I GO TO BED EARLY TO GET MY REST

All rights reserved.

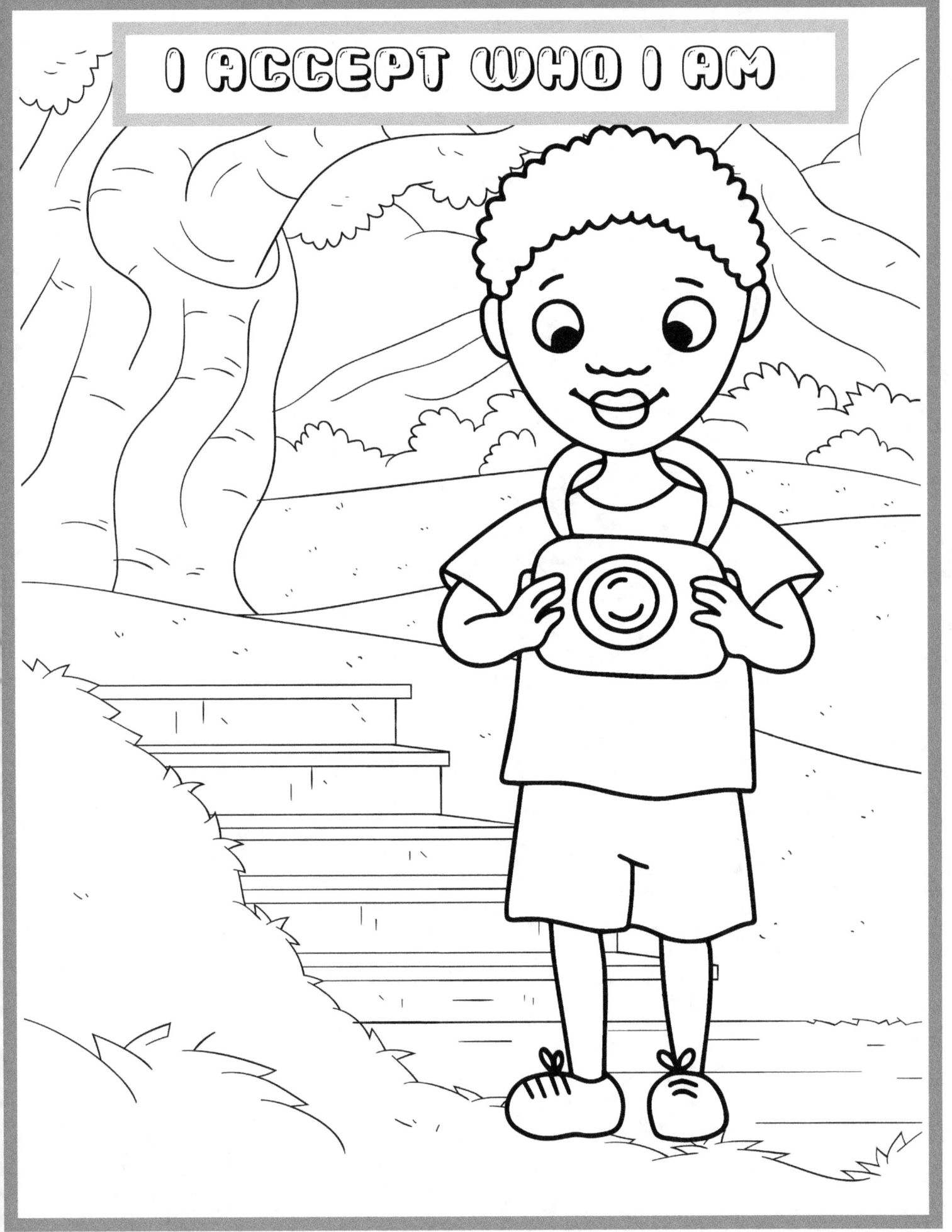

All rights reserved.

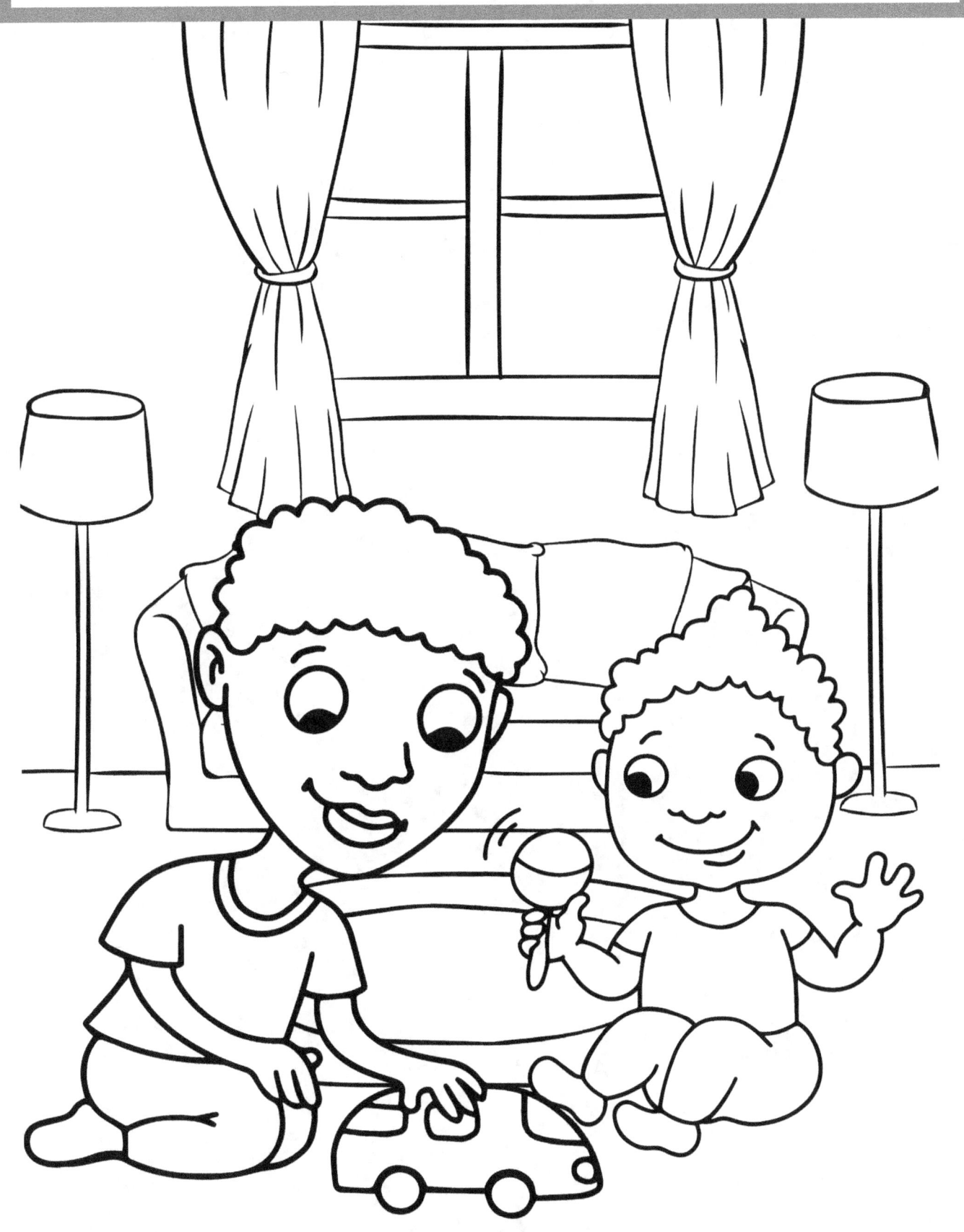

All rights reserved.

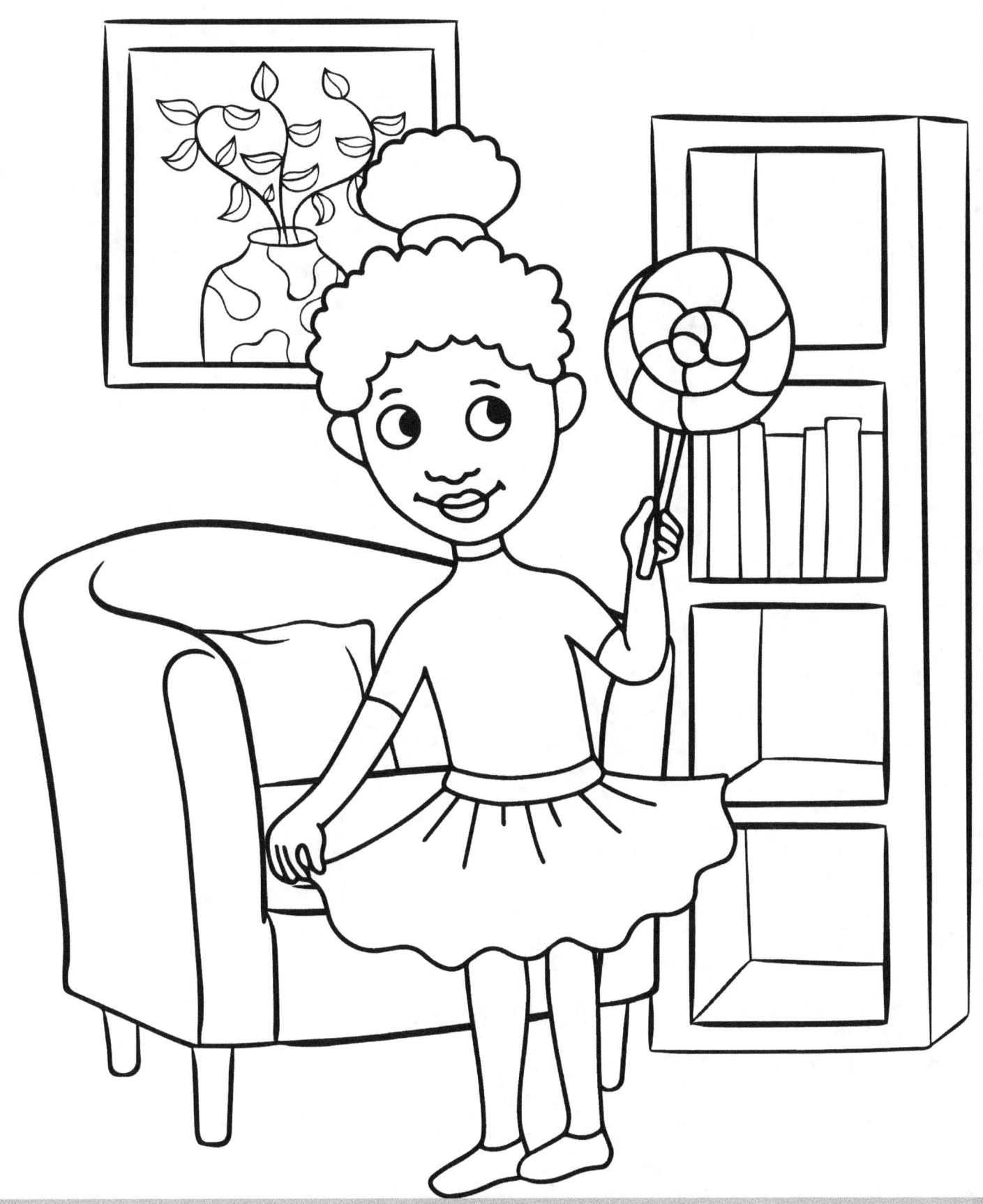

All rights reserved.

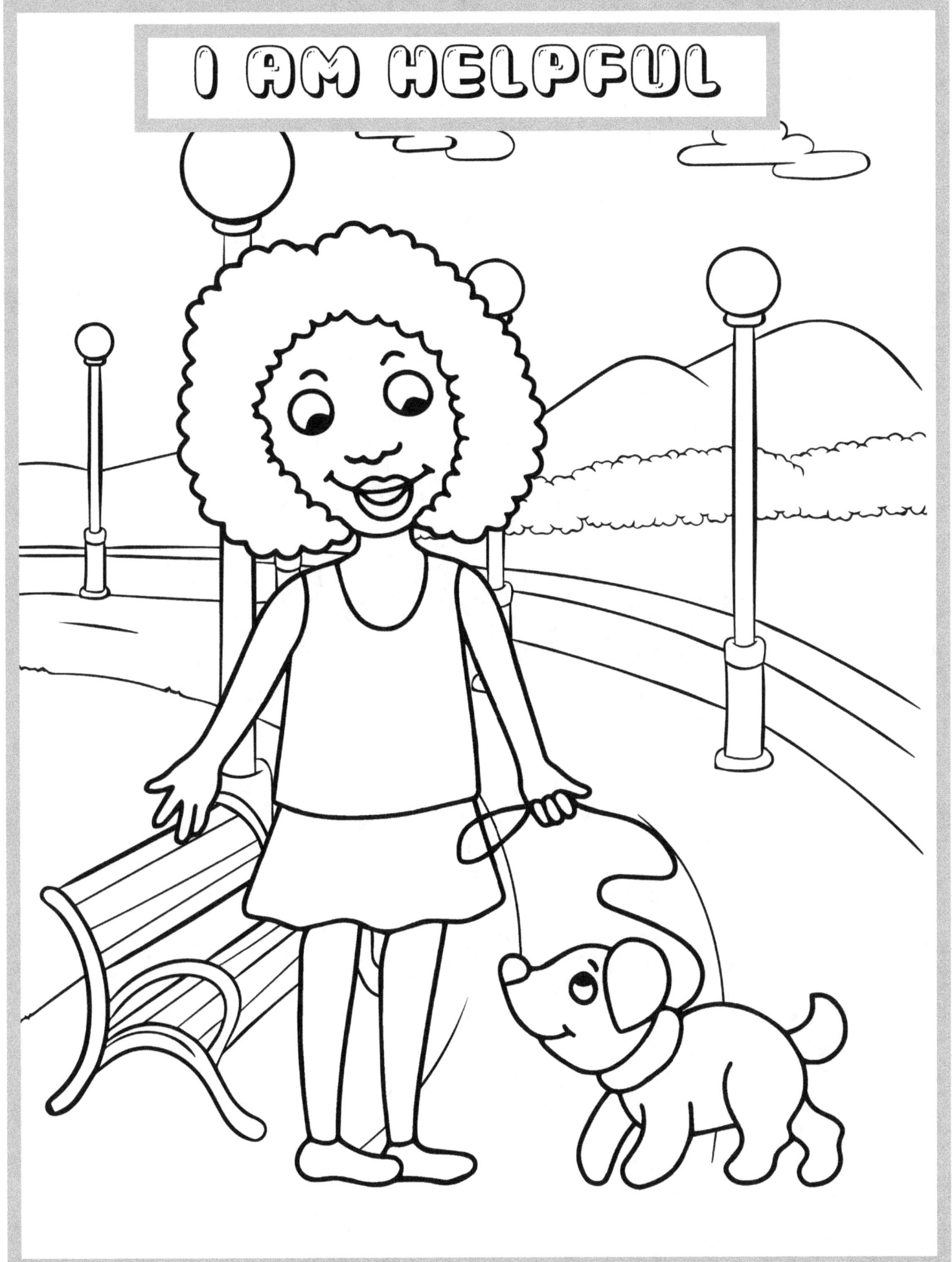

All rights reserved.

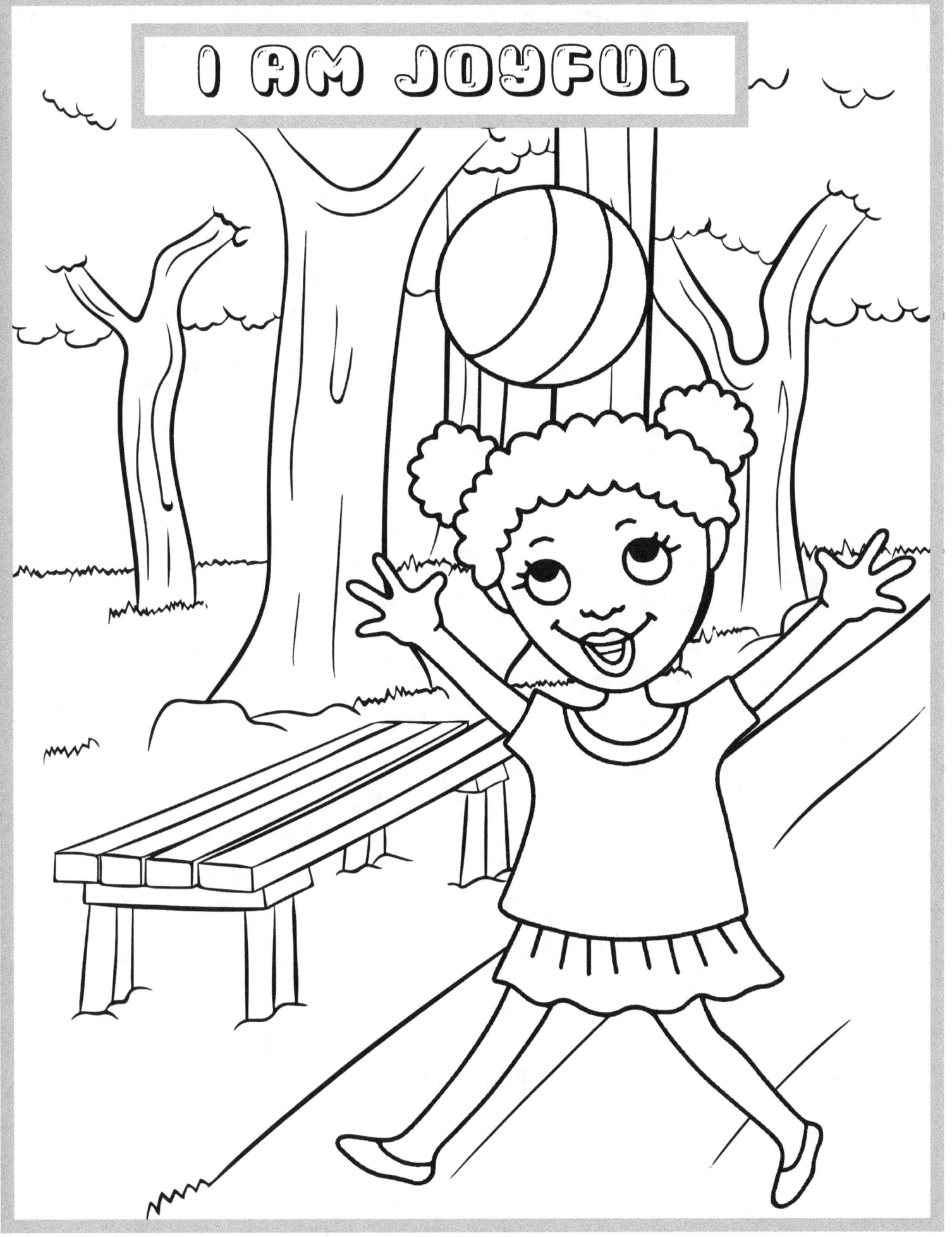

All rights reserved.

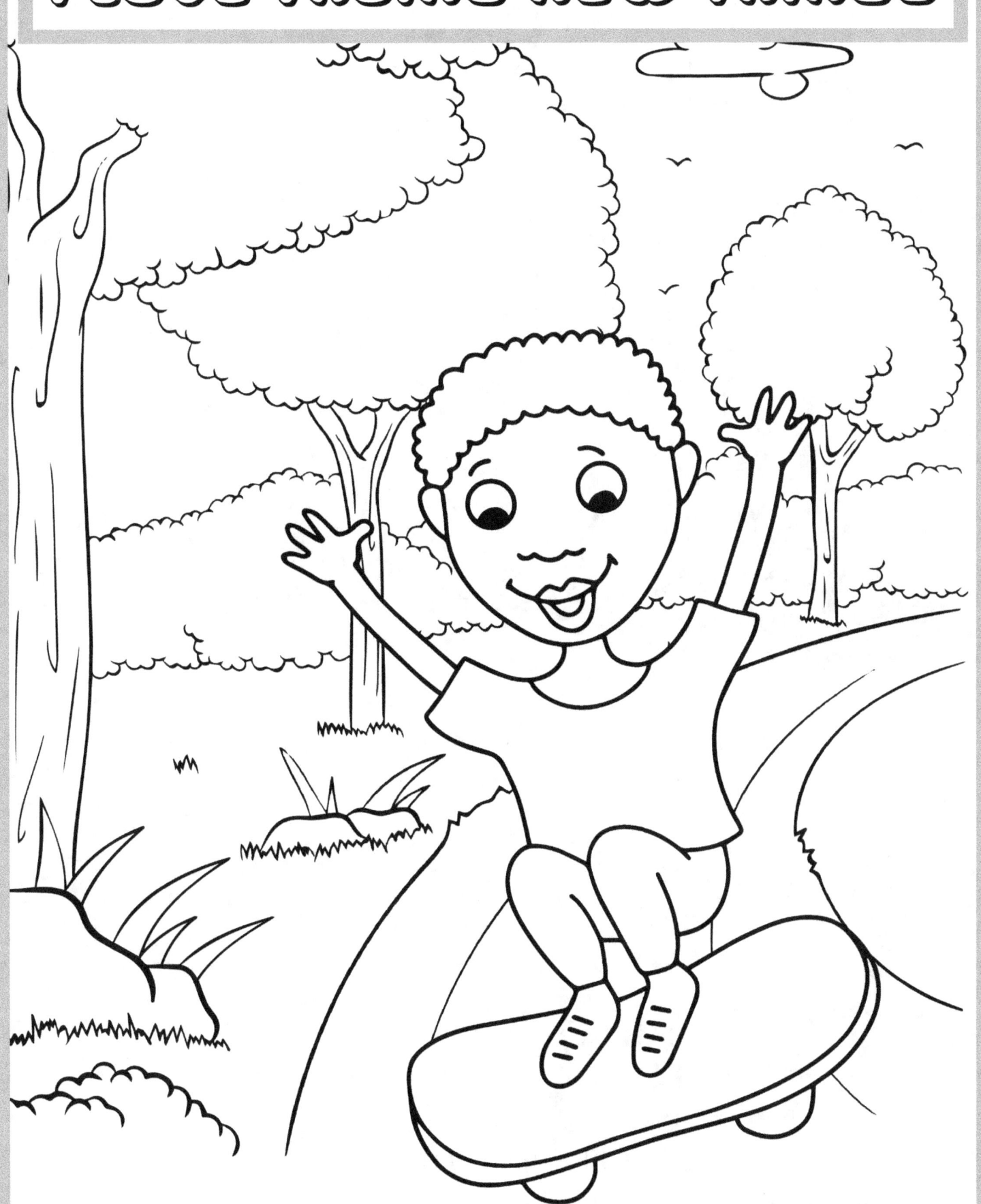

All rights reserved.

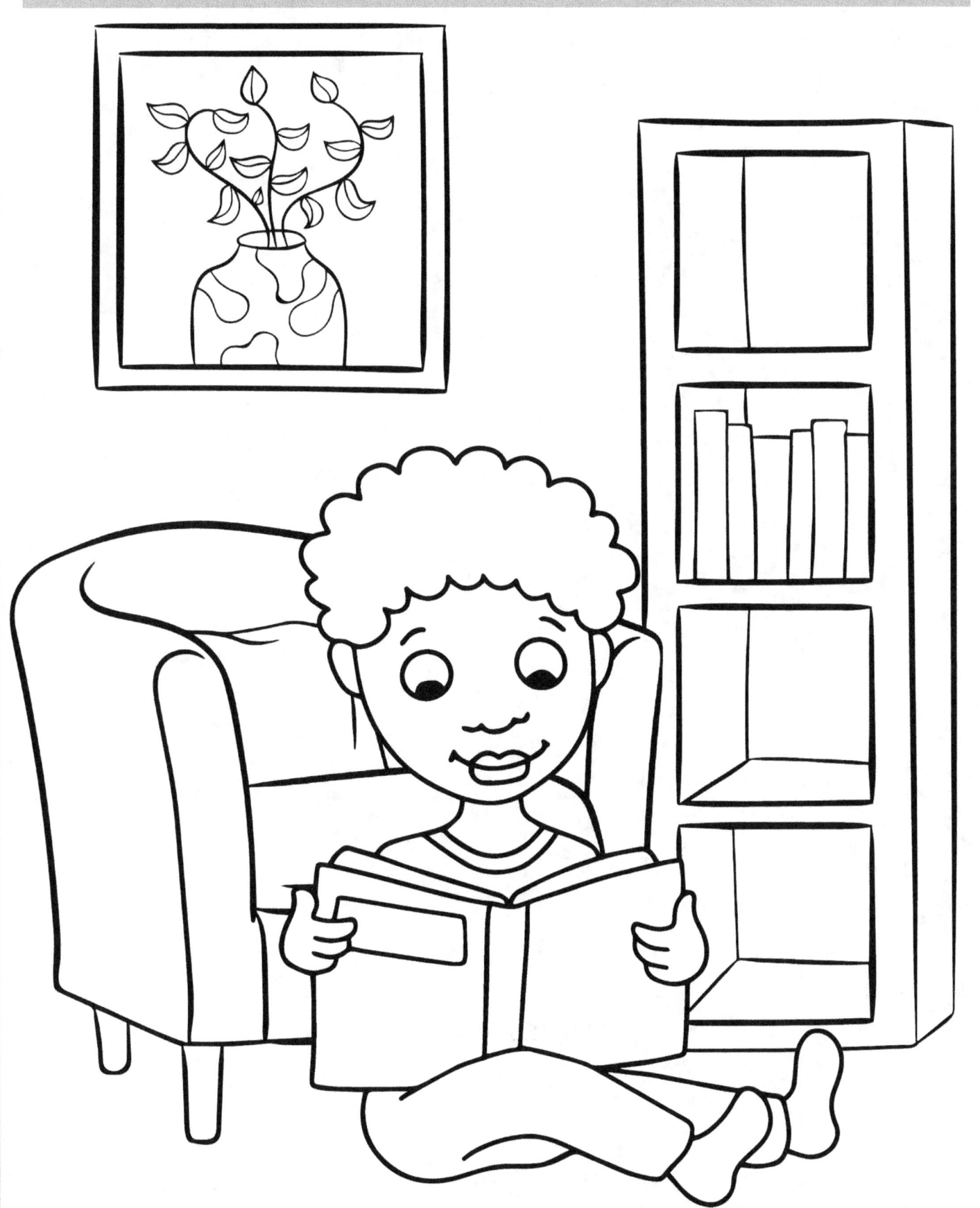

All rights reserved.

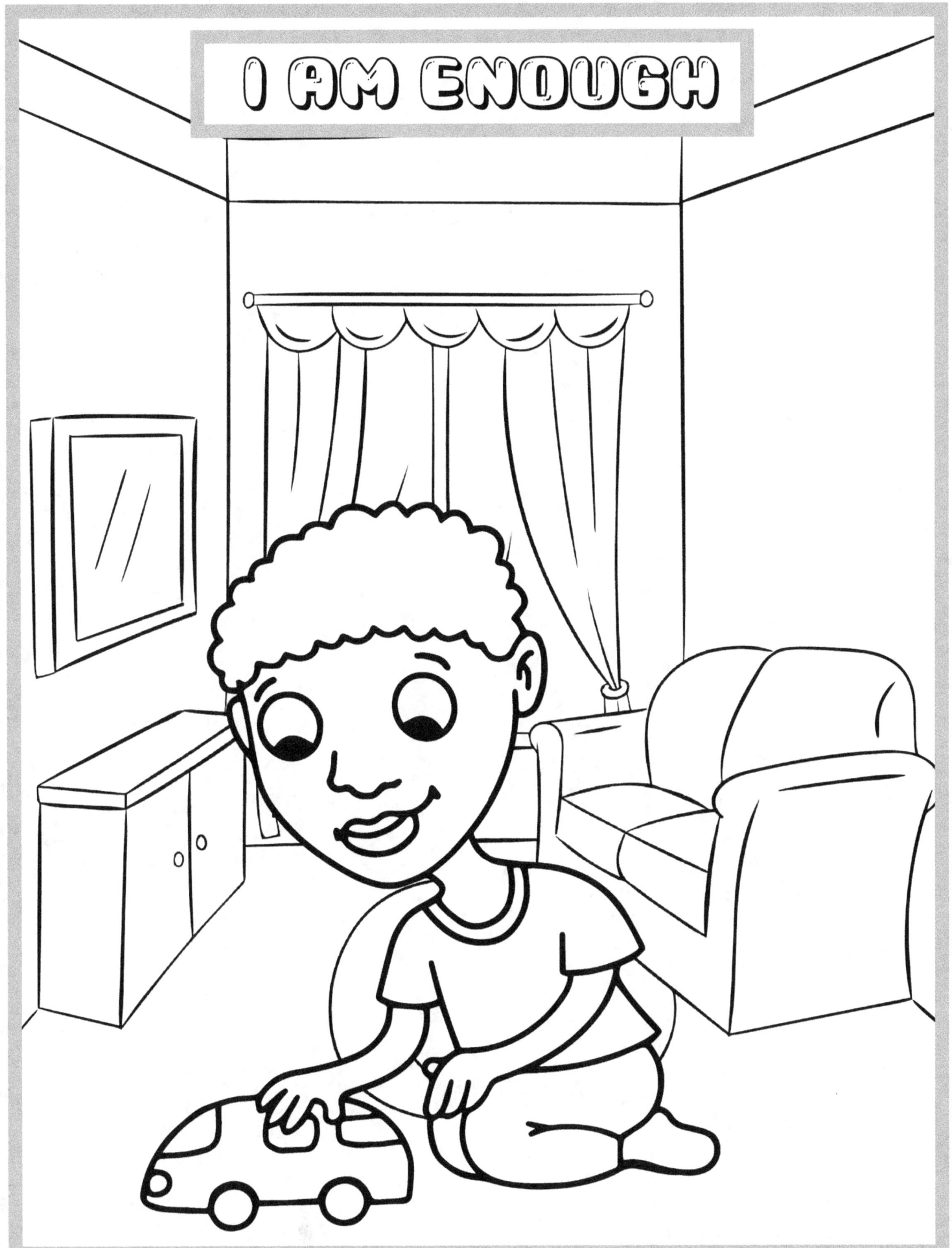

All rights reserved.

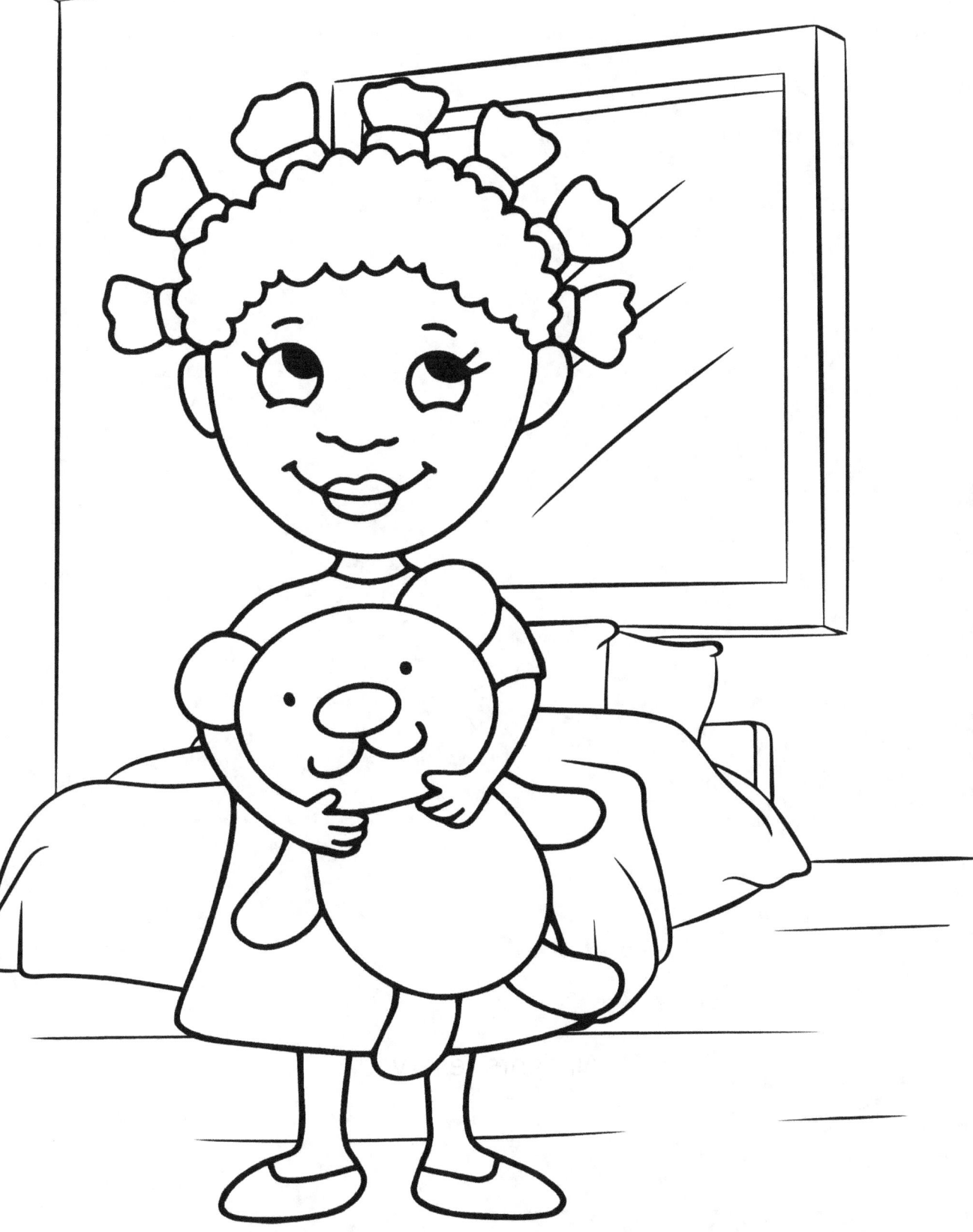

All rights reserved.

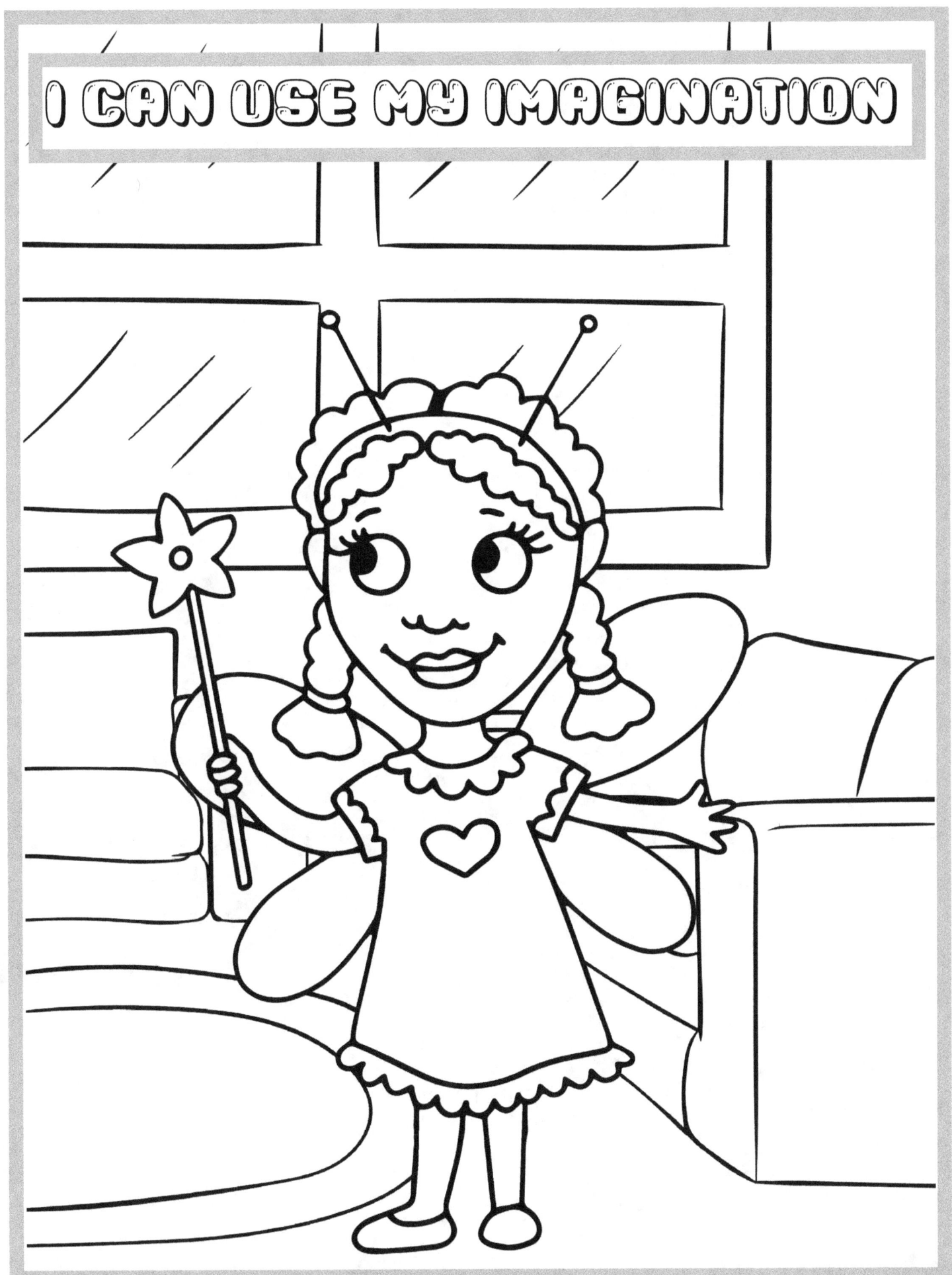

All rights reserved.

I AM KIND TO ANIMALS

All rights reserved.

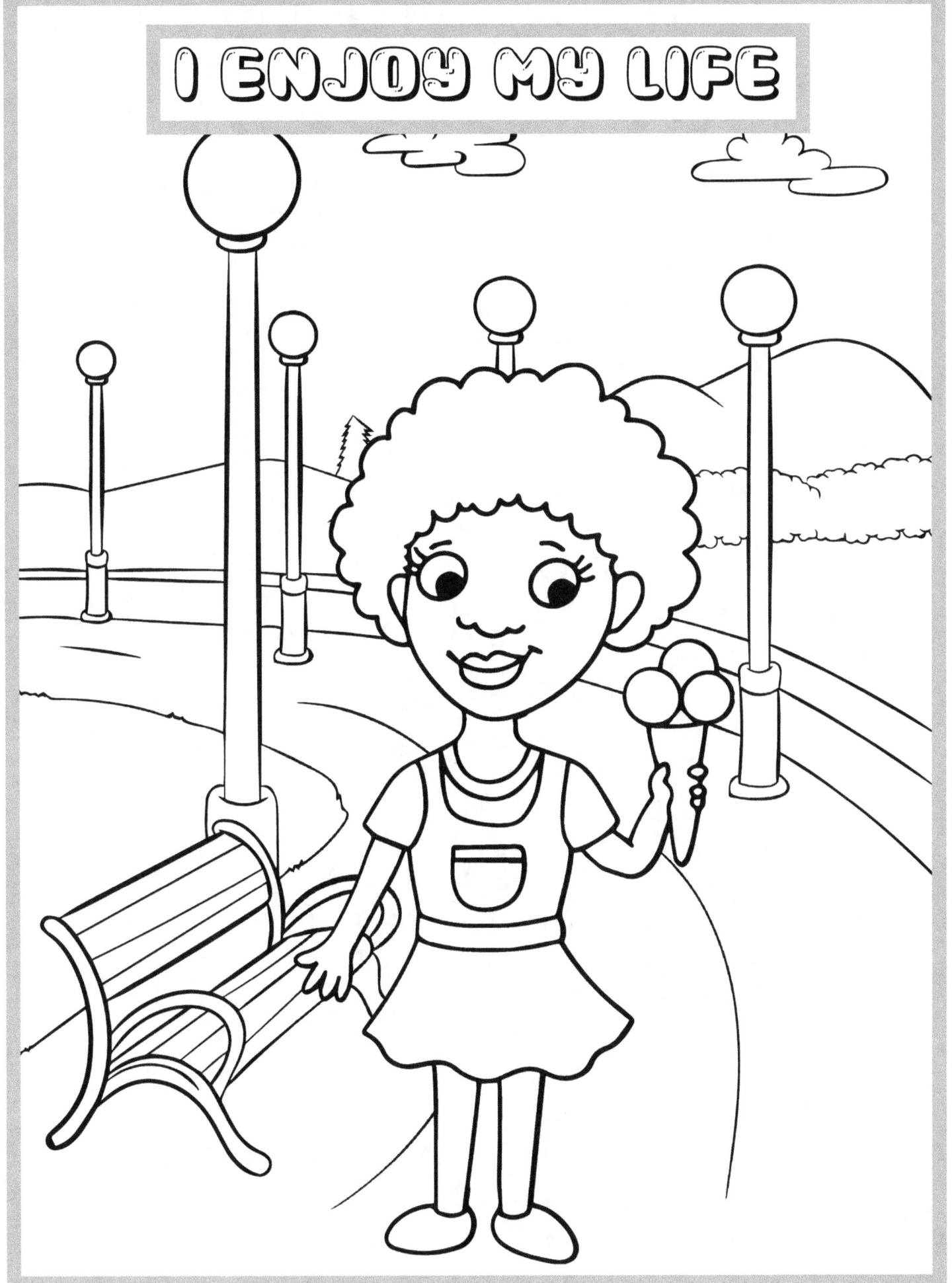

All rights reserved.

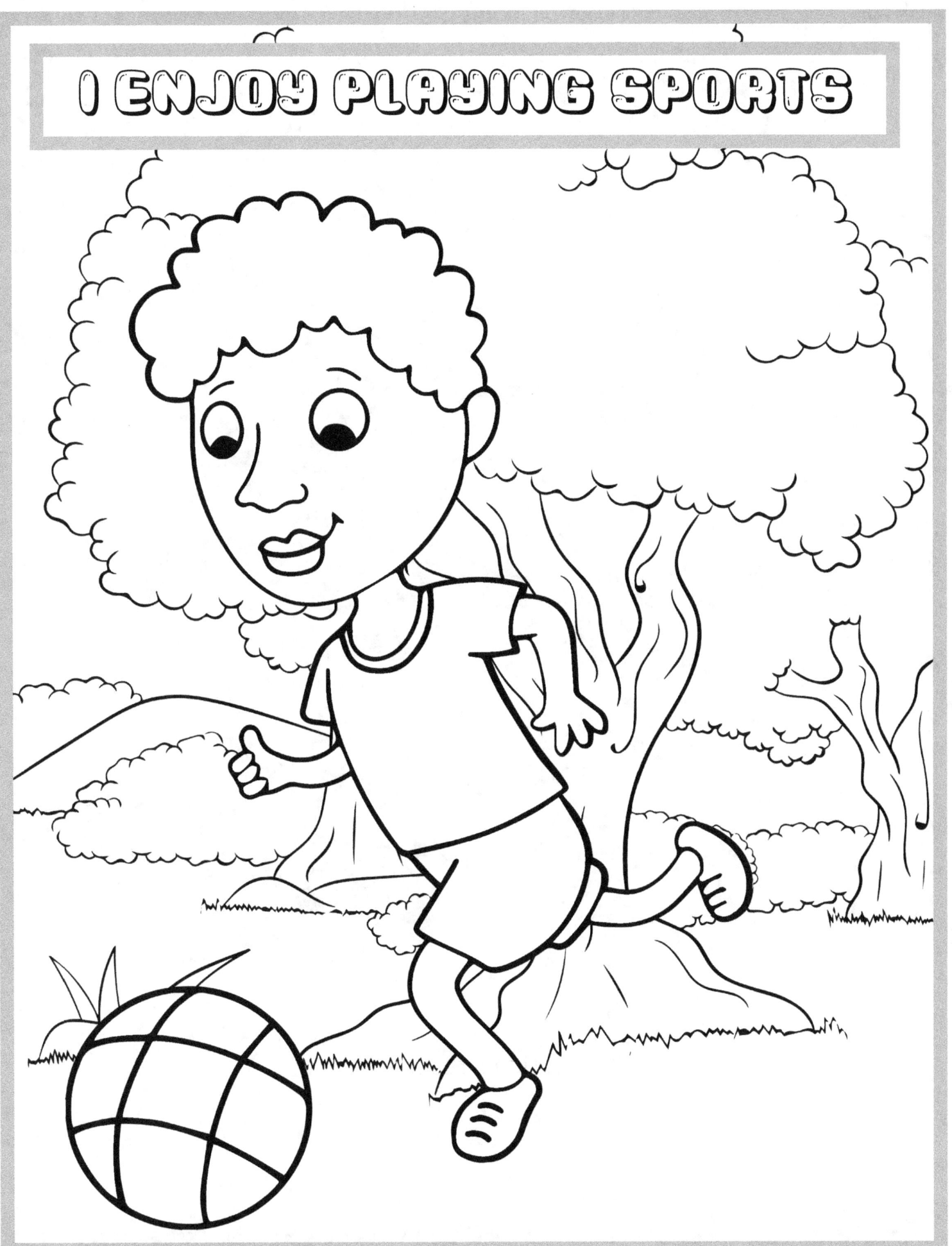

All rights reserved.

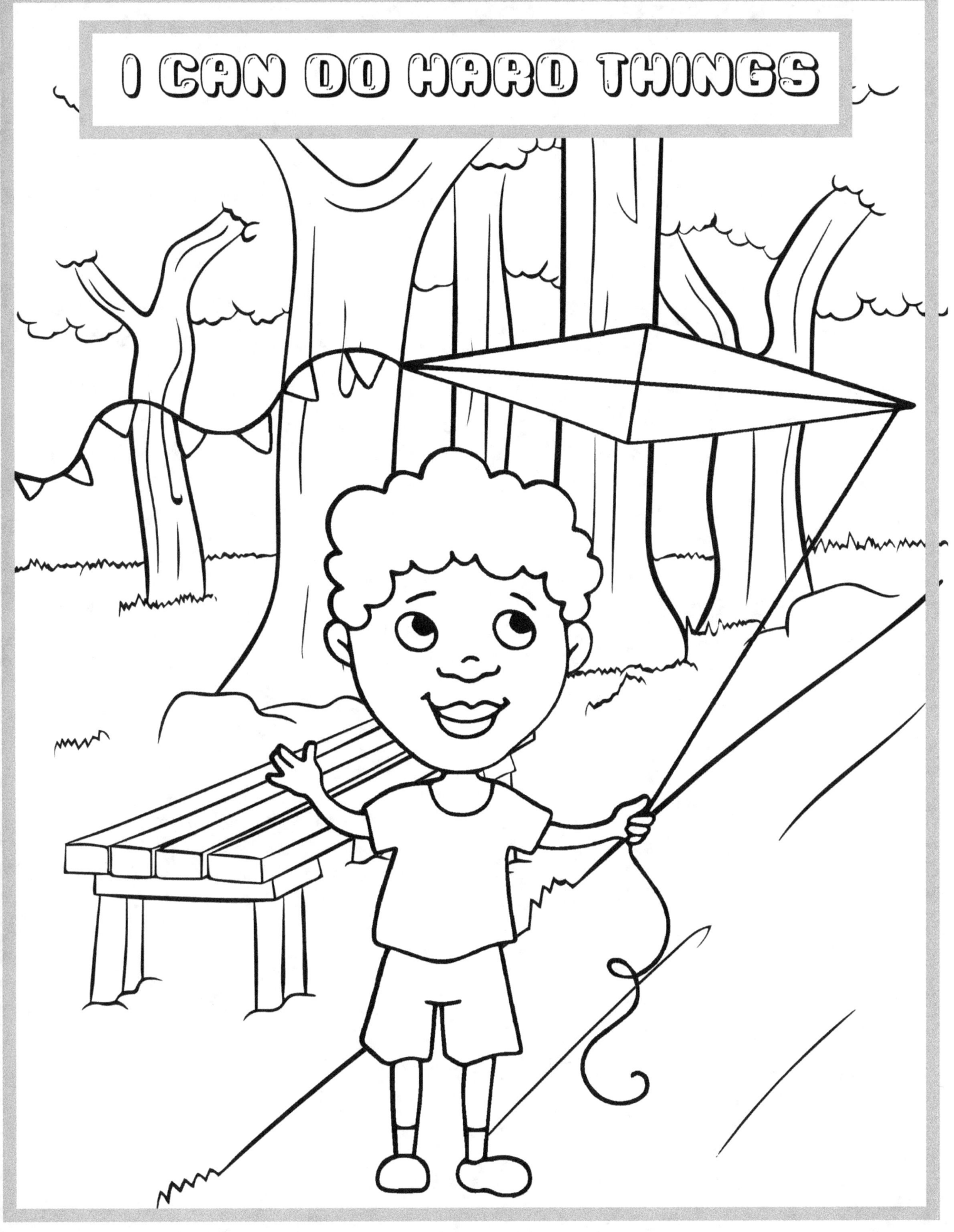

All rights reserved.